Llanto Tonto

POEMS: VOLUME 3

David Almaleck Wolinsky

DOS MADRES

2020

DOS MADRES PRESS INC.
P.O. Box 294, Loveland, Ohio 45140
www.dosmadres.com   editor@dosmadres.com

Dos Madres is dedicated to the belief that the small press is essential to the vitality of contemporary literature as a carrier of the new voice, as well as the older, sometimes forgotten voices of the past. And in an ever more virtual world, to the creation of fine books pleasing to the eye and hand.

Dos Madres is named in honor of Vera Murphy and Libbie Hughes, the "Dos Madres" whose contributions have made this press possible.

Dos Madres Press, Inc. is an Ohio Not For Profit Corporation and a 501 (c) (3) qualified public charity. Contributions are tax deductible.

Executive Editor: Robert J. Murphy

Illustration & Book Design: Elizabeth H. Murphy
www.illusionstudios.net
Front cover photo: Reserva Ecológica Costanera Sur, Argentina,
ca.2000 by David Wolinsky

Typeset in Adobe Garamond Pro, Footlight & Mythago Squares
ISBN 978-1-948017-94-7
Library of Congress Control Number: 2020941974

2 A. and not 2 B

Table of Contents

Awful
Author
Preface

Public figures give speeches in which they are "humbled" by this or that. Yours truly, though, was hammered to the floor when he realized that of all his work, this was the wrong book for these times.

Behind authoritarians and viruses ride the five "systems" horsemen. Don't know 'em? They know us. Despite its complex wonder, the human world seems hell-bent, taking some of the natural world with it.

Irregardless, I lift myself up and dust off my pants, and the preface:

Soon enough I will be 73 (probably). My "Early Poems" have seen printlight, if not readership. In its unpublished evil twin – *The Auschwitz Cookbook,* Poems: Vol. II – a few poems refer to events that gave rise to Black Lives Matter, and worldwide convulsion after the lynching of George Floyd. Our present President also gets a dishonorable mention. Other poems sing or scream unresigned to older sorrows and atrocities.

Thunderheads and dunderheads loom. This, my Volume III, has less thunder and more of dunderhead myself. Other works are in the works, based on shakey assumptions about days. A second wave of plague will come, but our "leaders" urge us on – in wishing and pretending otherwise.

Or, as Bill the Pill wrote: *These late eclipses in the sun and moon portend no good to us.* He chose to speak this through an old man who would later have his eyes gouged out by his son. See the last poem in this book for further Shakes-presumption.

And stay tuned if you are so tuned.

> – *David Almaleck Wolinsky,* June 2020

Prologue: New Year's Report

So nice to get your annual letter.
A hug would have been better
I think, but then again I think
so much these days that when again I think
it is of the friends who are not my friends.
Maybe I threw them away,
or was not so good a friend for them
to stay. It is possible; some would say that.
But fear in my heart
is that you would say nothing –
or shrug, or sigh, and go on your way
with faint, unpleasant memory – that I
have become that – and anyway we all have our own
lifelines and lives, entangled elsewhere.

Well, that's that.
It is more than possible.
Today is the first day of the rest
of my life without you, him, her, them.
And with the few, distant, who remain.
One said *All these years!* and another,
How precious is gratitude.

True: I intend to count
my blessings in a separate,
less separate, report. Perhaps
a two-part intention....

Meanwhile and always
be well, my dear. I surely
will see you, or someone, here or there.

PART I

Ai Lasso Mi

A Calendar

On Monday I see I am blessed:
grandpa, husband,
progenitor of poems.
Mi suegra Florinda
will soon be 106.

On Tuesday – See, I am cursed:
haunted, hurt, few readers
for my dumb lament.

On Wednesday
I trash my bipolar diagnosis.

On Thursday I forget what day it is.

The next day, awash in the living world:
Our cats, a caterpillar calendar, the night sky.

On the morrow I die
or I don't die.

Once More Onto the Beach

He wrote a hundred poems to everyone
about loneliness; he ran out of words.
He ran out the door.

What anyone heard
was anyone's guess,
but he knew, more or less.
It was less.

To Susan Livingstone

So, Sue, you like
my work most bitter,
two hundred percent agreeing
how fucked up is the world?

And now, after all these years,
you do not choose "Living" anymore,
having replaced No Exit
with Go, Exit!

It's your reverse Cordelia act –
nothing to come of something,
or maybe you and Bobby McGee,
born to win but left to lose, I'd say.

I love you too, Sue,
I really do: just not that way.

The Wind

The wind came in
at six a.m.

The wind
unkind
old friend
cold dread
blew in.

Intent, blown out.
Speech borne away
in whirlwind career.

There is knowledge here
somewhere,

orphan child of fear.

The Good Thing

The good thing, it seemed,
was four a.m.
when every road was clear:
By brilliant stars and pale moon
we weren't going anywhere.

But darkness gathered 'round five:
the rain, the mud, thunder in the blood,
rhythm of All Roads Lead,
footstep suck and wonder --
and good to be alive.

The Mariner

And as he sailed on,
his heart was fluttering
like a sheet in the wind.
He sent up the yellow flags.
He sent up the orange flags
and then the red ones.

(Dead calm.)

There was blood in the water
but it was not his.

There were garments – wet rags –
clustered near a sewer:
yellow, orange, red in the black gutter slick.

Night. I alone. Street lamp shudders.
Lighthouse beacon winks
like a glittering eye…

The Letter

ain't got time to take a fast train -- Al Green

Oh dear,
another letter
from someone you do not know
to someone I do not know,
delivered by dubious service
causing approximately
3.14 persons to be nervous.

Is that proportional?
Is that fair?

Fair is foul and foul is fair.
Hover in the smoke and filthy air.

Oh dear. Not mine. Shakespeare's
letters, his artifice.
I wrote to her only
Please read this.

You know the rest. No rest,
like some knight in Keats or Poe.
Some parched, sad place to go
with someone – well, you know:
someone you do not know.

Mr. Fear

He is not your doctor the true healer
who once had been a nun;
he is not your fifth-grade teacher,
witty-wise and still a mother
to all the kids in the class.

Yet he, his eyes dark and burning,
his long arms scary, fingers bony,
has come to teach.

You are not beyond his reach.

Song

She's in and out of his mind
like the ballad in an old man's dream.
He would have to be deaf and blind
to miss it, whatever it means.

Out of his mind.

Resting awhile here,
he will travel again a waste
in the company of love and fear.
The wind runs before;
rain streams down his face.

The wind, with its wordless song,
the rain and its wet kiss.
She will not listen long
to the pitter-patter, or this.

James's Song

My name is James.
They call me Jimmy Shit-for-brains.
I do not wear it proudly,
neither am I ashamed.
Each, it is said,
becomes what he makes
– no matter if waste or dust –
and gives back at last
what he takes, as all must.

James may now be beggared,
however he defend, coffee-
creamed and sugared
or buggered in the end.
Despise him not.
Thrust your hands in the dirt.
The certain hurt
will neither maim, nor mend,

but bears familiar name:
James
alone, unspoken,
no one's friend.

Llanto Tonto, *for Joel & Ahuva*

1.   Temps Perdue Chicken,
Temps perdue, cordon bleu,
who so freakin' nuts to try
and thread the needle of the past?

Which. Was that?
The one where grandma's family got gassed?
The one with Turgenev
discovering First Love?

and so on
and go forth;
who went forth like the moron
who would be beloved idiot
and got it half right:
was not content, was not
uptight. Dostoyevsky maybe,
Tolkien, Shakespeare and Schubert.
Dufay or Dylan? Both,
but not too bluesy
when the prowling wolf
howls to himself.

Past: no book, no record.
Passed: the train the station the river,
the thought
off the wall off the hook off the shelf.
Old man. No one. Lover.

Who knew, O my beloveds,
what abysmal cracks open
between *care*
and *dare*
and *prepared?*
O beloved rhyme
my joint out of time.
O give me a home
with buffaloes,
friends, guitars, Budapest
string quartet.
Lend me your ear
your heart
with interest.

Come by here.

    2.   Rule of Thumb
Thumbs up. Thumbs down.
Live or die.
Go to town.

The rule of thumb
is, When you're done, you're done,
and that is that.
And that is… what?

That after wrangling valiantly
and less than, you are done with wrangling.

The sponge squeezed out,
bones grown stiff,
the Big Easy is diseased;
you go no more a' roving.

The rule of thumb is that a pen
is not held between thumb
and index finger, but by those two
and *up yours.*

The rule of thumb is
that when you are Donne
you are not dumb.

     3. Terror
How go there which is
here, *terra poetica,*
terror incognita, terra terror,
where heart and head and hand are bound
in mortal error?

I thought just now of my dead sister,
of how there is no j*ust now*, but now
I see your long-ago faces,
and think how then and now
they have shadowed each other
in a man's mind.

He cannot ask forgiveness, whether
there is nothing to forgive or not,
only repeat the stupid knot of words: *cannot,*
ask, give, love, as if there were
ties in this very hour, now,
to untie.

Will you abide
them? Him? He also
may forgive
into nothingness,
hold his own
that is not, that is his end
in a windswept conversation
and echo-chamber of years.

Now what syllables
will rhyme right here?
Not terror. Not tears.
Danger waters....

My Cousin

Angel said
it had not spread.
His wife, *not so.*

She spoke with calm,
not like one
in fire, where she must go.

And he: *Post-chemo!*
I am a strong young man,
as you all know – and a Fighter!
A fighter.

I wish I could say this lighter.
It is not disease
has broke my grammar.

Brother life, sister death.
Not Angel. But his wife,
and not only she.
It took away my breath.

Who knows?

Who knows?
Set
a word
down
by the river
side by side,
one
against another,
syllables
by eyelight,
slight gleam on water,
dark, wet bark –
last light, weeping
from the trees
as it goes.
You, who knows.

Darkly *(Am Bach im Fruhling)*

Is there always a 'B' section?
Is every third modulation
an ambiguous peregrination?

You said it
about Schubert
and said it
and said it
and forgot what you meant.
You said Reddit
and never knew for shit
where you read what it was.
Your mind tried to edit;
it fled instead.

Standing on the corner
watching all the girls go by
you were not dead.
You were afraid, darkly.
You were looking at
your own head, and it
was a mile away.

There is more to say,
maybe, but Forget it.

Must it always be this way?
Ruthless, sweet counterpoint.
Light on talking dust floating
through the door, *chiaroscuro.*

Open-Source Love Letter

Darling person,

You would not, I think, be too shocked to see
after all these years how I've gone to seed –
and you won't in any case see me.

I do know this, in a formal way,
not quite unreal as realizing
we do not live forever.

But if I was a carpenter
I would try to remember
that this is only a song.

And if I were a moonshiner
who couldn't tell elixir
from he licks her, you can guess
where that would get them, or me.

Or maybe you can't.
Better the devil, you know?
Our deal went down without Bob Dylan
or Bob Moses, or Hadjidakis or Chani, or Susan.
Nobody's home sang the voicemail, *it's over*,
but I babbled on ardently, Babylon
and the Forest of Arden on fire.

Are poets liars? Outliers? Outcasts? Doubtful
lovers part-timers rogue rhymers all-
of-the-goddamn-abovers?
I would say *Don't be ridiculous*,
except it is.

Like when he wished the girl on the train
would move over, so he could sit next to her.
He hoped. Moped like a Bronx teenager,
all flowery and rattletrap, until
he falls asleep, and doesn't know it
when the clattering deserted train
rattles to the last stop.

Once

Once there was a boy;
later a boy still, and a man,
and an old man, though not a very old man.

When Percy Shelley cried
then what is life? stranded
on an isle of joy and misery, his poem
and the poet who asked were all,
all exclamations of a still-young life.

Franz Schubert asked; he answered
stepwise into his last sonata,
fading *andante* to nothing, soon after.
They said his name was writ on water,
when all that remained was music,
wisdom of a too-wise youth.

The hand that traces this
is an unsteady hand.
The man is a boy is a man.
Once – a time less, a time more –
he thought he knew the score.

Once. And again. What was that?
In sinuous line the worm turns
beneath a wheeling flight of stars.
Once and again, time upon time,
and then, like those lights in a warp frame,
he will wink out.

The bird in the hand

The bird in the hand
and the two in the bush
confound logicians
and metacognition,

because what is
is not -- as often as not --
and realistic we suspect to be
turd disguised as word.

How then might we live?

That is a horse of a different color,
and a bush inside of a bird.
Nor would I go there if I could
except for something Uncle Archie said
about green leaves, a wood,
and wind on water.

When I was a boy
I was Archie's daughter.
Nothing wrong
or surprising about this --
just angular song
that sings of what is.

Mechanical Failure

When he had a poor grip
with the plumbers wrench,
he changed it for pliers
and cracked a chrome collar.

Oh, for not holding off.
For doing what he couldn't.

Now he must wait
in twisted regret
for a skilled workman
to worry the connection out.

We would not disappoint.
But of things
and power over things
there is no end
to breakdown,
no failure too small.

Memento

Desiring a girl,
you see a grinning skull.
It's not, you see,
what you thought it would be:
White on gray, on black-gray, razor
outline, unforgetting face.
What the heck, you say,
it's what I get; I might as well
wear it 'round my neck. You do.
It's like that old song *The Weight*.
It's like nothing you ever…
Man, do you ever.
It's like nothing.

Ultimatum

You better do something.
You better come up with something.
You better something something.

C'mon. Hurry up.
Time's running out the window.
Time's flying out the door.
Someone
kicks you to the floor.
Want some more?

Better something.
Something or other.
Something. Or else.

Heedless Suite

1.

The deep, Quixotic longing
that discovered Rumi's America
and simplified trembling Quakers
could make, perhaps, *Israeli*
rhyme with *humility,* and swell,
we imagine, the sap of every tree,
drop by molecular drop.

2.

Hopeless love
and loveless hope
are hapless distractions
and ridiculous distinctions.

3.

Slice my eyes.
Turn up your drippy nose.
But put on with me the morning,
this morning, of heedless words.

4.

No mere rumination
on arrogance of nations,
when dust-throated indigenous
pronounce this. Or so
you might have heard; something
has stopped our ears
all these humiliated years.

5.
What is sentiment
and what the sediment
of history?
What aspire
into refining fire?

I could perhaps know,
who – like all – shall go
from welter of world's woe
into infinite dust,

but I fear I will not,
neither you.
A debt is paid;
another comes due
as it must.

Bronx Buddhism

I am attached
to the cat who is not attached.
See him there on the mat?
He knows how to sit; I do not.
If I look long and soft
into his green eyes, I might
disappear, or become otherwise wise.

It is clear:
Watching, being watched,
I will not be scratched
by that cat. I will keep
my vigil, and later his breathing
will measure my sleep.

I tried, I really did,
not to want him to stay,
not to watch too hard
as he crept away.

You already know it:
When this cat died,
I cradled my face and cried.

Half of an Autobiography

This hurt.
That hurt.
Some confusion,
lasting pain.
After a time: anger
and the house that anger built.

There I lived, for more years
than some persons have years,
before I thought *There is a world,*
probably, elsewhere.

And looked.
And walked around
more years.

Sometimes I hid.
What I found,
what was learned or earned,
is not written down,
nor what else I did.

Today in History

Where was I today?
What did I do?
The dishes got done;
the laundry was streaked with blue.

A Swede saw a city in a cloud.
The mailman cursed aloud.
Mail was outlawed.

Swedes who kept watch in Sweden
saw Voltaire arrested in his garden,
caught with his pants down.

A million women marched,
a few of whom were men.
I was one of them.
Was rain, and camaraderie.
It was not today

At homely Bible study
Jason proposed that we
were friends of a single mind
as apostles came to be.

Did unbeliever I
believe my gentle friend?
It didn't matter.
I knew where I was
for a minute, then,
which was not today.

Where I was today
I cannot say.
What I did
is hidden.
I remain unbidden.

FacelessBook

I've not sufficient likes
for commerce with y'all.
I may be lost in fact
to anyone at all,
though I have many lives.

I leave you to make sense of this
however so you must. I will return,
as Joni said, to carbon; for now,
just talking dust.

I've heard that this is wrong.
I don't insist, except to say
it is my song. Will it persist?
How long? I do not know;
I know no other way.

I read your poems, Henry, again last night.

I read your poems, Henry, again last night.
Again. I know: we grew apart.
But still I could not think it right,
the years as friends, then not.

Nick Aquino died last year.
You did not know him; I, not well.
I did not know until this hour
the mark he left on me.

What passes, passing before us?
Children, children lines, treacherous
wordings. I know not to what end
the hours press on, or what of them
a man might need to know. But stubbornly
backwards have I always delved
and sought to know, my friend.

Weather, for A.

Dancing in the dark, puking
in the park, I never knew
chasing memory
of you, how little would I lark

chasing, chased,
by delusion pursued.
Nor for sure how nearly erased.

Now displaced, plainly
defaced, unembraced, I wander
the limberlost without regret.
It's just – I do not forget.

Storm of ashes. Blind
worm. Startling spark.

The Rabbi's Daughter

What great fortune
to encounter the rabbi's daughter,
hold her a moment, be-
held. And after, to travel on
without, seeking within
the soul of love, the soul
that loves. So one day,
then, to turn around
and miss fortune, find an end
to wandering, loving, everything.

To an Old Tune

Here is a start
that finds no end,
that will not mend
a hole in the heart,
and yes, we may die thereof.
Yet it's love that begets us
and does not let us forget.
Love, begetting love.

Here is a spirit that has no home.
Wear it so ever close to the heart,
it wanders; it wanders far.

Love that impels us
through Hell and fear, it bears
no other name (*quick! rhyme!*)
Love. Love that we are.

Through a Glass

Oh pumpkin-flower
my never-daughter,
how I have longed for you.
How you wanted a father!
And look what happened…

Look. It is better to.
Better, even, than being read to.
Better than being read,
which you do not like,
or being liked on Facebook
which you do.

Forgive me my bad jokes,
as we forgive those
lost in the bad chokes of longing,
estrangement, ignorance.

Give us this day our daily Love,
as God, in whom I do not believe,
has given us children.

As we look into the eyes
of your beautiful babies,
see what is left for us – what will be.
Que sera? We will see.
Face-to-face, my child, we will see.

DonnaBeth No. 1

What we learn, difficult.
What we learn, beautiful.
For all we learn, we are grateful.

Whatever we learn, it is not enough.

So we learn, yearn and burn
and turn at last to laugh
at plain inadequacy,

which makes us a little free.

Then one day the horizon:
black, wall of water,
tsunami upon us. Then
not free, unready, we learn
the thing we cannot name.

Then *the wind and the rain*
indeed. Then turn, turn, turn,
turn again.

DonnaBeth No.2

Skillful means
are worth a hill of beans
which could, after all, feed a town.

The problem, it seems,
is just what that means
right now, as the deal goes down.

For not preparation
nor alienation
has brought us to this pass:

Beneath the great gray sky
Pachamama Tierra
her scorched history
and yours, truly
flat on his dried-up ass.

Control~z

He was a confused, and confusing, man,
which meant, betimes, *forget him as soon as you can.*
Yesterday would do just fine

Lately no matter the omens are grave,
the sky black-gray, the sea
boiling to a cobalt blue.

No matter that lives
are dangling by a thread,
and that thread, somehow, has searched out you…

No matter no matter
we natter, searching and searched to our rue,

who stumble and lurch,
fail, recoil, touch
as we may one day
renew. Another – *undo*

Toccata, BWV 911 (Marc Edwards)

With or without.
Could Glenn Gould save us? How about
The Nuts and Bolts of Cults?

Epistemology for Dummies, yes?
It was I guess more-or-less
Beethoven Opus 13, then,
you at a baby grand – from there
to the Goldbergs and back again,
from Molly to Count Kaiserling
with many dotted half-notes in between.

What is my theme?
Was a person I knew –
whatever the tense past means.
Is a person
or two, now, for what Time's being
writes, demeans, remains for two@70.
One: So distant it could be the Moon
or Robert Mann or Schumann for all I know.
The other: myself presumed I know,
but in truth – unknown, this one; unknown
the Other. Whom I thought of, once
upon Time's black staves, as my brother.

The ABCs of A.

Remember the time we went down to the Village to see
"The French Connection"? And after we walked arm-in-arm
on E. Something St., and the next one and the next,
until store lights faded and memory stumbles in darkness.

You don't? It was less than 50 years ago!

Okay, maybe not "down" to Greenwich Village.
Alex and I went down there from the Bronx
(*to pillage the Village*) but maybe
 lovers left from a walk-up on Atlantic Avenue.
From the Brooklyn, you could say, that I never knew.

Which might be a part
of how I got to here, apart
without a prayer,
a man on the knees of his heart;

I'm not sure....
Make... break...
It's sort of a wrench connection,
the rusty tool
of a klutzy old fool,
and stuff you never mention.

Past Perfect (*for Sam the Tailor*)

What Ray really meant
What Charles lost his head over

When Casey Stengel Jones was young
the old Yankee Stadium was young
and the boy who rode the No. 4 train
was just as not-guilty as any other
Unknown Citizen of the Empire State
who wanted a chance to scream
Kill the umpire! and if you still
didn't like the call, according
to the next day's *New York Post,*
well, you could just go down
by the riverside, and watch the footballers
kill themselves, or go **** yourself
if it came to that.

Enough.
Someone nuts enough.
Someone enough.
Tree at last, great **** almighty, tree at last!

De Profundis #65

I give up now. Or I don't
though I want to. Or just want.
And waste, knowing not
more than whatnot.

The foot has always
been on the other shoe – now
a boot that batters me 'round neck
and head, hands fending uselessly

though I am hardly dead
yet, nor any blood externally.
It is a pummeling still.

To remain still as a mouse
before the stalking cat
might for a time forestall
headlong dreadlong flight
to cancel, if possible, the possible.

But what would then remain?
Pain, merely? Disability
in slow, concatenated train?

No answer. Just the world
dragging its dead ass to a bad end,
and you for the moment scanning this
blue-gray array, my sometimes friend.

I Would

41

I would, you see, know
what has become of you.
You not memory,
melody, mythology, misty
or wistful guess.
Please bless
this

poem thrown over
invisible wall.
Overthrown.

Wanting
to be known.
Found wanting.

Bless curse this mess worse
I confess but tried
to make my voice, small.

Llanto Común

      1. Stranger and Friend (*A confidence, for DB*)
And why confide in someone
never but briefly met?

An answer, in part:
I am an imaginative cat,
imagining confidants.

Else a lonely cat
limping around what he knows not
like some drunk Harry in an alley.

That may be it, exactly, or just
how curiosity skills this cat --
not all that, and not all that just.
But in trust we trust
because, it seems, we must.

Is that enough? *Enough
is enough!* I hear.
It is, I fear.
Or more than. Depending
on hunger, the ratio
of skeleton to fur,
of face to face,
and sometimes liminal
grace, step by stealthy
step, stealing forward.

2. While We Lived, *for Edna*

While we lived
things
being what they were --
but Lord, they *were,*

which leaves, as the sun
singes autumn's fringes
and frosts, its mark.

We were
what we were --
if it were not
we, then some kid
me, must not
have understood.

While I lived my wish

was you, not lost,
only to let me know
some, you

who lived
(I do not say loved)
and lives.

Now it is winter.
A beggar ghost breathes
against frosted white.
What is the most

a crystal spirit may ask
or wish for? And how is it
that in reckless quest
wishes live, still?

3. To Two or Three Too Many
He was not the only poet
to have drifted into your orbit
nor, in most senses or even
senselessly, intimate,

but, like Pluto now
un-discovered,
less than planet, some
distant chunk of ice
consigned by cold astronomers
to categorical darkness.

Her Name Upon the Sand

He wrote
as who, should he be
thus stricken
all his days,
would not?

On the granular littoral,
in the glare
of airy nothings.

And if you see nothing
but dunes, sailors,
jailers and failure there,
there is no shame --

only further night-failure,
blank sand blackness
and that vast namelessness
without name.

A Marriage

      1. Your Idiot-Knives
You always kept them in your back pocket:
Handy, and not hidden.
I married you anyways.

Regrettable battle.
Predictable blood.
Defensive wounds and otherwise.

And good whittling when it will,
more-or-less. But *a fiddler's life
for a fiddler's wife* still,
I guess, will not say all.

      2.
I was your big tree.
In a moment of anger
you called down lightning.

You can see now
how I am cracked
open, and the black char;

you can hear in the thunderous silence
storm-angels singing no longer
above the blasted valley.

3. A Big Fat Anniversary
Thirty years: Intimate
argument, intimate struggle,
raucous fracas.

Now a fine *how-you-do,*
to do with less: a piece
treaty treating less wholly
with my soul, your soul, the unholy mess,
us.

4.
In her sleep I could have
kissed her hair, sat up and walked away
forever, but I was not in her sleep.
In my wake, from which I cannot walk,
I live forever and a day; then I die.

I got up and hunched beneath
the kitchen light to put this down.
She slept on through the night,
untroubled and unknown.
My waking self – waning
and alone – sits here and insists
on one more minute
to get this right. I will not.

5.

An old man slept
by the side of his wife
nearing, perhaps, the end of his life
as the night waned
and the day ran on ahead of them.

He could taste the dark and silence,
breathing through the half-light
as the moon slipped slowly by
and dawn came roaring on.

Watchman, what of the night?
the brief, tremulous cry.

Morningstar blinked with the eyes of the dead
and the day, my love, ran on ahead,
and the day ran on ahead.

Juan Torres, *for Ann Taraborelli*

> "My heart is my compass" —Juan

1.

Tall and skinny, Juan looked good
in those charcoal pinstripes,
un torre elegante for sure,
and yeah it was cancer
that came and smeared a charcoal shadow
beneath his eyes.

Yet I think he knew karate, because
he angled back his boney frame
and knocked the killer backward seven years.

But in the end, it was the end.

2.

I had been a friend, and then
I was somewhere else,
kicking at something else.
Too late to become one again.

Too late, too late.
Others who loved him bore his fate.
I live with that. I wrote down this
a year later. One more
graceful man to remember,
angling back farther, farther, almost
lazy, as if it was easy. Until it was not
and he could not.

Nothing, then,
but to love him here,
love him gone.

Get Over It

It doesn't happen; you do not.
But the heartbeat oscillation
between misery and plain pain
rests, I believe, in the latter.

So batter my heart, motherfucker, no matter.
Some recourse dwells
beyond reason or belief,
beyond grief. It will not shatter

though hurricane blow bitter
against blasted limbs
and strip them, leaf by trembling leaf.

He was a friend of mine…

Jerry was
unto others
too, but to
those Krishnas
unmanageable devotee,
later unnoticed
casualty.
Collateral homage.
(I too did not see
the end of that rope.)
Jai shri!
Jerry.

Epilogue

Everybody knew the words were birds;
everybody knew they flew.

Everybody knows everybody's
no one.
Someone had a shotgun.
Gus had a blunderbuss,
Guinevere a spear.
Marissa was pretty pissed.

An albatross dragged a holy cross. We
are not permitted to touch too much
on this. Birds on that day, they say,
just flew askew
into a nightmare of flies.
Poets as usual were telling lies,
and picking their feet of clay.

Everyone knew
what no one said:
The legions of the dead were on the march;
the sky was turning red.
The only chance
 -- no time to put on pants --
was Get out of bed and remember

something unspoken
not broken, some
small puddle of sun, seeping
through a window where someone is weeping
on sentences no one has read.

Mocoso Redemptor

The little snotball wishes not to be
overly honest. Ignorant, he still believes
he knows too much. That if you knew
what he knows, could you ever love him?
Say hello?

But then again lately
I've been thinking what I thought
was not at all what I thought.
Owl wrong. Pell-mell. Or maybe

slung sidesaddle on a racehorse,
or the dog would hunt, but askew,
racing through the brush in some houndish
mathematician's drunkard's walk.

Now how
about that! You know,
I intend to keep on,
one foot misleading the other,
without knowing how.

Likewise my next breath
unless of course –
until, of course –
Well now it doesn't much matter
what I thought to say, does it?
The next sweet breath
has already kissed
my tender insides
on its way out.

I'm out of here, said the youngblood.
Said the wiseguy: *No doubt of it: I'm out of it.*

An Old Couple

There are two of us,
a sprained mess, but that
will not always be the case.
If this is obvious
is it any less tearful? careful?
dreadful?

*This, that, this, that, this.
One, two, one, two; one,
none.* Tenderly, dear,
or overdone. Here and gone.

An Old Mother

One minute she was sleeping,
the next, dead.

A minute she was leaving,
next, had gone.

There is much to be said
for either understanding:

Here, there. There, here.

Neither lends a commanding
view into the chasm

where commands disappear.

The little broken cat lay on the rug,

The little broken cat lay on the rug,
struck not by the big dog whose ears
she was wont to lick, but by time.

Time breaks all, someone said, and why
should anyone listen to someone? But I did.
As she lifted her head, mewed,
dragged her body behind the old chair,
I listened. I had to.
I was glad to, and not glad.
Petting her, imagining
some thick violet life-force flowing
from my hands to her scabby tabby self,
I thought *Life can touch life,* and then:
Life can lay down beside life.

I was not right or wrong,
just miserably relieved
to fit caress into song.

What traverses a stricken cat
could be akin to a howl seizing a baby.
Unnerving. What good in stroking
her gray matted hair? Why not go
to the store, the hairdresser,
to a wedding or to war
while the little one creeps
out of this bad world?

But like a gutted lighthouse I kept watch,
fixed on a foundering patch of gray, there,
the loosened sinew, the striped, matted fur.

PART II

Forty~One Etudes
& Bagatelles,
Op.69

Weary of being

Weary of being
a marvel of a know-nothing
or a wary upstanding something
outstanding notwithstanding
one in such perdition – landing
on his feet?

Sweet. So what, if he
were we? That is in question:
Whether it is nobler, or not.

Our lot. In Sodom,
in someone's jaundiced eyes.
In Eden and in this
imagined gangsters paradise.

In That Case (A Preface)

In that case I would have said
something reasonable-sounding,
after you had spoken your part.

No permutation
of misfortune, however,
could have changed that
which, in the event, was not.

In its place a hard case
and no place for the likes
of me, but yes
I up and went there.

I would like now to voice something reasonable
about this, that, or maybe another thing,
but in any case, stubborn alien, I do not.

In which case – nonetheless and not
revelation – you are free to ignore me
but not free.

Scribbler poets wish to skip the worn grooves,

Scribbler poets wish to skip the worn grooves,
skip through the brain-ruts and dance
like raindrops inside you.

When Hell beckons
the tempo quickens.
And when Death
opens its maw, With grace
or with luck, shameless I declare,
it is a door.

The Nutcracker

Springs are loose like a wild goose,
wires are gangly like a boy.
Though digital wizadry traces the face,
it seems an unsprocketed toy.

What is it? What is it?
We 'd like to know!
Your loud, sputtering cry.

And so, my dears, would I.
But I'm lost and a ghost, at the Christmas show,
like a partridge in a pear pie.

The Misanthrope

He's a moron – she's a moron.
I am lonely drinking boron.

She's a psycho, he's a narco.
I am lonely and loco.

He narcissist; she masochist.
I lonely and won't be missed,

who was born on a far planet.
No one believes it, not even you.
Everyone knows it is true.

Born thereunder a bad sign,
I never met a stop sign
I could abide, or vice-versa.

Then which is worser,
your shit or mine?
Is there any damned thing
I could ever abide?

Words, words, words.
The answer is words
we agree to deride.

Going in Circles

"He's sad," they said.
Except they did not:
There was not "they"
to see that, no circle, or few
to say it to.

In circles of its own
his mind whirled on and on.

Étude 19 (Tu Fu)

When sleep fled
and the roof fell in,
what became of the man
and his twisted bed?

He holds his head
in trembling hands.
He is whirled away
to unknown lands.

Fidget Spinner

What's with it, round
hypnotic fidget,
spinning his eyes
around – surprise! – your eyes?

This is so satisfying,
said Maria to her mother.
What could I do? I agreed.
I gave them, all shiny, another.

Etude 1.5

Sleight of hand
Fate, at hand,
in the bush
in the rush
of sound, memory
– rare bird –
too, and how
can I keep
from singing?
my little
history to you

Grace Note

Everything fits.
How easy everything sits
on a chair, on the floor,
wherever vagabond footsteps repair.
Yes that is it: I am, for a semi-quaver, repaired.

Windgrammer, for Kathleen Parker

Didn't you know, you
dirty comma-nist, that this
administration has it in for
whistle-bowlers, just like
some editors for uppity women?

Seriously, deliriously,
how dare you pray, tell, write from wrong?
But never mind:
your piercing parsing
is wonder investigation, which has –
like this singsong song –
gone on too long.

From the Swedish

God Jul.
God save the queen.
God bless America.
God blast Amerika,
you'll
understand.

(Song 69)

There is not enough rage
left in my old age
to push one foot before the other.
Funny, how I hear you say
There is another way
as I crawl out beneath the weather.

Nothing to fear.
Nobody here:
not Bonnie, Diane or Heather.
Nothing is clear.
He went somewhere
on his knees in the mud-swept weather.

Étude 11

There once was a dreamer named Lou
who trod on a stone in his shoe.
The stone or the dream?
he wanted to scream.
As if anyone knew.

The same old gentleman Lou
quite often wanted to screw.
Concerning consenting
he was unrelenting.
Screw you, too, Lou.

Rhymers aligning their rhymes
lend mettle to unsettled times,
they say. So they say. Who *they*?

Go away now. Go far –
or stay, reading between
unseemly seams,
innoportune visible lines.

On the Naming of Cats (Étude 12)

I adopted two
whom the shelter called Chips and Pringle
as I could not abide.
For his paws I named one Dactyl,
and the other, Fractal, to rhyme.
My wife calls both of them Rectal.
Woe betide.

Shamble Fish

Sits on the floor
like lox on a dish,
and they call him
shamble fish.

Walks out the door
almost never.
Is running a low-grade fever.
And yes he forgets to wash, sometimes.

Shamble-fish, shamefaced fish,
like a forlorn demon's
forlorn wish.
Never to shiver and flash -
just shamble, stumble, flounder,
and sometimes a muffled crash.

The Mission

The mission – short on remission,
downright remiss or an evasion
of necessary humility we surely
are wiser to not mention –
plodded forward, dragging its mortals in tow.
Work, yes. But as if a comical
and beautiful insect – a mantis, say –
was praying on a leaf and behind it a storm
brewed into holocaust, here is a green
stick-figure bending to its task, within
a cathedral of shadowed leaves.
And look: silly missionaries crouch in position
like snipers at the treeline, not scenting in the wind
the question What will be here tomorrow,
in an hour... in the next second?
Although we do not know,
we are guarded and misguided by a sense
that we must go on. That the mission,
whatever it be it is what it is so be it,
becomes you, and you the mission: tentative, insistent,
obstinate. Trembling in shadow. Not to be denied.

Bathroom

The guy in the mirror said to me:
"I know how much you want to be free
of what you are and what you see.
Well what you see is in your eyes,
and what you are – likewise."

"Talking mirrors could never be,"
I observed to a square of white tile.
The mirror cracked a smile.

Employment Étude

You didn't sign up for this job?
No you didn't sign up for this job –
not when you were a child
or when you became a wage-earner.
Nor did the kid
in the Australian outback,
or the Syrian one.

What is this job
you did not sign up for?
No one has signed up yet
to tell anyone that.

Worse

Once I had a stroke.
Once the bloodwall broke.
It was *Nightmare on Night Street.*
No joke:
It was worse.

I just wanted to cry *I die.*
It was no lie
or evil prophecy; it was worse.

It was not a curse. I was not lying
at the bottom of a hearse.
Still I began to choke.
I would not break, or croak or wake up --
just hurtle from hurtful to worse.

The Pianola Bar

The perforated music
unravels at your feet.
It is not bitter, not sweet;
it is stained with Rheingold beer.

You wobble out the door,
but will not get far. You are all,
after all, that remains of the pianola bar.

Trumpet Tune (The Art of War)

> *You're in the army now.*
> *You're not behind the plow.*
> *You'll never get rich*
> *you sonofabitch:*
> *You're in the army now.*
> — song my father taught me.

You're not in the army now.
You need it as well as a cow.
You want to be rich,
you beanstalk bitch,
not in the army now.

You're not in the army now.
You don't even wonder how.
You scratch where you itch
you SOB
not in the army now.

You're not in the army now.
All I can say is Wow.
Or maybe Ditch!
I don't know which
army that is
"over there," wait: near,
advancing ruthlessly now.

Art of War, Ch.3: On Strongholds

A fort
shrifts short,
inadequate bastion.

Its soldiers do not
soldier on; they just do
with you or to you.

But a fortress, understand:
A fortress
slags out into the stress in force,
repels insurgent aggression.
Stands strong.
Stands long,

black shadow over the land.

None Drum #1

Was it chaos?
It? Well...

Down the well fell Alice, toward none, no charity at all.
Rabbitrabbitrabbitwholesumparts,yesyet rabid, PG-13
Wonderland: The Movie. Beta. Or better not.
But butterfly net worth it!
Safety. PIN. Net? Inter-not. Cloudsourced.
For sure. For sore.

Unearth it. Up-hole it.
It? Well. Very well, indeed. In thought so.

Autobio Ditty

Ate some dirt
hugged some rocks
did what could
to take the shocks
the hurt:

One deluded out-of-place
mote on the face
of planet denuded
by predator race.

Little boy lost
in grownup lies
unskilled to live
unready to die
when he can he cries.

Kissed some gravel
down in the dirt
dreamed with Sister Maya:
Still we hurt, and rise.

The New York View of Rooks

How could I have knowed?
I grew Bronx, circa
the Middle Ages: long gone
into places money flowed
and money fled,
and in the cracks, survived
as always, never the same.
Derivative?

What:
Castles? Corbies?
The New Scots Review
of old *nu-zhe*?
Wall Street *bogatyri*?

In Jersey today
two gulls flew
into current air.
Not an eternal pair, but still
tracing the same sailing.

Rooks. Rakes. Schnooks.
Pendejos. Cakes
and ale. How munch
a month? What price
mortgages? Cosmopolis
of street-dancers
and cloud-hoppers
reading books and decimal points
in the shadow of Beijing.

Funny thing
about that, about war,
about carbon, litter,
literature
and all the myriad synaptic
roundabouts still firing
formerly priceless Lehman PhD's
needed to drive this little piggy
to the market but untrained
god nose to discern
ironic points of light among
collateralized damages and other dark matter.

Out of Hand

It was never a bird
or two in the bush.
Just something heard
on a musical vine,
that ripened beneath an obscure sun,
chirping differently to each and I swear
they meant no harm, those heedless words--
whatever they are not worth
to humans and their hill of beans
on the old, long-suffering Earth.

About Last Night (Song 84)

What happened last night?
What happened today?
You gave me a fright.
Who went away?

This Is Your Life
was a TV show.
The story since then
it is hard to know.

The song since then
it is hard to sing:
the music, the night, the rain;
laughter, disaster, everything.

Étude (Of Course)

Of course
the question is *Why?*
The answer
a cipher.
And yet, and yet
we try. We try.
We live, undergo, die;
go under, through,
around. The sound alone
is din and thunder, unknowable
but not unknown. Ears.
Like years shot with doubt.

Do not ask
What was *that* about?

What then how then?
Why then?

Cry, then.
Cry out.

It was not exactly true

It was not exactly true
that the fabric of his life
was the thread he wove at night
with an inky stick, but it seamed so.

It seemed sew.
When he could not weave,
he labored to breathe.
And what tatterdemalion
patches might he live?
He did not know.

But to counterstitch,
align, pull density and intensity
from chiaroscuro —
was a lifeline.

Weft and rhyme
warp of time
note of many colors.
Child of mine.

WTF

What?
I, die?
And you?
Uncle Murphy?
Cousin Sue?

The FedEx person too?

WTF
GHI
JKLMNOP
QR-SUV-XYZ!

I took too long, you say,
to reach the end.

Too soon.
Too very soon, my friend.

On the Late Works

of stalwarts and jerks.
All the criticism, wit,
talk *about,* ventures
at speaking *with.*

Alone in a room.
Brooding. Scribble. Dribble.
For us, too, late.

The Rain

It was teeming. The rain, that is. And he was dreaming
(who was making this) in hope it fall and fall
like rain into eyes upturned in some good turn
of events, one that deserved another, as we would
deserve each other. Would serve. In a world, that is, that
is not.

If time and the rain healed all,
some crust might sometimes wash
off malice's monumental glyph.
But this is dreamy stuff, the stuff
kind fools are made of. As is
this damned fool, aligning, carefully,
syllables to slide from a white page
like breath into unimagined air.

The hopeless white project

The hopeless white project
of putting one foot before the other
went on apace:
a bug
on the blazing shore
creeping into shadow in the shadow
of the ocean's green-gray roar.

Works and Days

Oh my goodness
and my badness,
just an attempt,
unjust, to say something
with small sadness
about something someone
otherwise unknown
saw.

It is an old saw,
a see-saw,
a whipsaw and
a coping and a figure saw.

Such fools fooling
with such tools
never knew how rotten rules;
others have forgotten.

Such a flip
saw, but my heart sore
and still I would know
(wouldn't you know?)
– before the jig is up –
what I have written.

Henry

How he arrived Without
Mythologies, I never will know.
No. Not thinking fast,
not fever slow.

I fell to my knees in the driving snow,
and waited for whirlwind to flag to a breeze,
for demons to eulogize Poe.
It was hours and years before I could rise.
But I swear to you all by Sam Hall's damned eyes:
Ages must pass, before I may go.

Llanto Mojado

Whatever I gave
you did not keep.
What pain, how wise
not to weep.

A breeze wipes away the rain.
A gray-eyed man
waits for dawn
again.

Llanto Frio

Where did you go?

I'm not sure I know:
Black rain. Driving snow.

The twisted streets
that ease a twisted heart.

Pitter-patter. This and that.

Walk apart.

The Grasshopper

Hop! Hop!
I can't stop…

Oh this is so
silly: wobbly
earth, world
elsewhere, but I
just jump and run,
jump in the sun

and sometimes over the lonely moon.

If there is, I mean, nothin' jumpin',
how is anything known?
It's an ill wind that is not blown.
What mean to remain?

Jump! Jump! I am no chump,
but I have dreamed of the fabled ant,
home-schooled and loam-schooled
how he granular moves
in a loveshine of sun.

But I – because I could not stop
for winter, for a prairie fire, for the high
hawk, they kindly swooped for me.
They were he, she, this that and the other
thing I was going to tell you after
I could smell you, but it got
forgotten – and then, I think I was eaten.

Help! Help! Stop.

Minute Waltz #2

Well was he or who or I writing something,
or fighting something?

Were we working elusive sound,
or just fucking around?

Jiminy Cricket

Jiminy Cricket,
the kittens killed it
or him, as your case
may be. Pink, they,
in tooth and claw.
I say no more.

Postlogue: At Ophelia's Interment

1.

What ceremony else?
No ceremony else?

Laertes jumps in.
Hamlet jumps in.
They tussle, those boys.

Wouldst rage and rant?
Wouldst cling to what dissolves?
How we love the gibes and the skull.
How grave, as all revolves.

2.

Oh my sister Susan!
Dead these fifty years and all that time
I write these kling-klang songs
to your shade, presuming
Shakespeare's shadow. It's funny, really,
how he lends the cloths of this world,
ruthless, some fabric softener
fablesong
for the live, and the dissolve, our revels ending.

ABOUT THE AUTHOR

DAVID ALMALECK WOLINSKY has had a chequered non-career. Highlights include 6 years of middle-school teaching in the Park Heights ghetto of Baltimore, a novice at age 47. Grandpahood later. Lowlifes include 3 volumes of unpublished poetry.

The Almaleck in his name represents his mom, her parents, and their lineage from Al-Andalus, Muslim-ruled Spain. His Sephardic ancestors had to leave their homeland in 1492, at the completion of the Catholic *reconquista*. He also answers to grandpa, and sometimes Grandpa Whiteboy, participating when he can in the Poor Peoples Campaign, 350.org, Jewish Voice for Peace, and Levantate/Rise.

David, his wife, and his *suegra* Florinda, 106, live with two cats in central Maryland. They share a small patch of earth with the birds and the trees, rhizomes and other critters.